Susie Nelson's Business Builder Books

Book #2

How to Book Parties at Vendor Events

Fill Your Calendar with Ease at Your Booth

by Susie Nelson

Copyright © 2016

Susie Nelson
email: susie@susienelson-training.com

Income Disclaimer

This document contains business strategies, marketing methods and other business advice that, regardless of my own results and experience, may not produce the same results (or any results) for you.

I make absolutely no guarantee, expressed or implied, that by following the advice in this document, you will make any money or improve current profits, as there are several factors and variables that come into play regarding any business.

Primarily, results will depend on the nature of the product or business model, the conditions of the marketplace, the experience of the individual, the application of said principles, and situations and elements that are beyond your control.

As with any business endeavor, you assume all risk related to investment and money based on your own discretion and at your own potential expense.

Liability Disclaimer

By reading this document, you assume all risks associated with using the advice given in the document, with a full understanding that you, solely, are responsible for anything that may occur as a result of putting this information into action in any way, and regardless of your interpretation of the advice.

You further agree that the author cannot be held responsible in any way for the success or failure of your business as a result of the information presented in this document.

It is your responsibility to conduct your own due diligence regarding the safe and successful operation of your business operations.

Affiliate Disclaimer

From time to time, I will promote, endorse, or suggest products and/or services for sale that are not my own. My recommendation is ALWAYS based on my personal belief that the product and its author will provide excellent and valuable information or service. This may be based on a review of that product, my personal or professional relationship with that person or company, and/or a previous positive experience with the person or company whose product I am recommending. In most cases, I will be compensated via a commission if you decide to purchase that product based on my recommendation. In some cases, I will receive the product for free for review purposes, or just to use. In some cases, I have used that product to my personal satisfaction in my own business.

IMPORTANT: Always Always ALWAYS do your OWN due-diligence before making any purchases, whether I recommend them or not. Never, EVER purchase anything that you cannot afford. Avoid purchasing products that do not have a clearly stated Money Back Guarantee, or that promise ridiculous results, like "Getting Rich Quick". Most people don't do anything with the products they buy, and most of the time, their results are zero – kind of like that "ski machine" that I bought that is now serving as a clothing rack... No, there is no such thing as a "Free Lunch". Don't do drugs, stay in school, etc. Be safe out there!

ISBN-13: 978-1539816119

ISBN-10: 1539816117

Why Susie Nelson is an Expert in Direct Sales

Susie Nelson has coached and trained thousands of successful home party and network marketing consultants.

Her students have:

- Built Million Dollar Organizations
- Earned Promotions and Moved Up their Compensation Plans
- Earned Company Incentive Trips
- Made Significant Increases in their Commissions (often doubled, even tripled their commissions in just one year).
- Coached, Mentored and Promoted Leaders

Now it's your turn! Dream Big - Believe in Yourself - and Anything is Possible!

To access more of her complimentary training - simply go to:

DirectSalesDaily.com/books

Be part of Susie's Facebook Community by "liking" her page, search for:

Direct Sales Daily

Get on Susie's email list (new product alerts, free training, and more):

DirectSalesDaily.com

Now - let's get your training started! Because…

I Can't Think of a Single Good Reason to Build Your Business S-L-O-W-L-Y
- Susie

What Business are you REALLY In?

Often when I'm out speaking with groups of Home Party Consultants or Direct Sales Consultants, I will ask the group,

"What Business Are You In?"

I'll get a variety of answers.

"I help women look and feel beautiful with a fabulous skin care program," or "I teach women how to cook with ease with cooking tools and utensils," or "I help women instantly change their figure and look 20 pounds lighter with our shapewear," and so on…

I could go on and on. These consultants have always practiced their 30-second commercials for networking events, and their answers are smooth – almost robotic.

The problem is – for serious business builders – their answers are all wrong.

The business you are REALLY in is the "lead-generation and sponsoring" business.

That doesn't mean you aren't out selling your products or services. But if you're a "serious business builder" and want to take full advantage of your compensation plan; then your strategy should be continuously generating new leads to work through your "system."

Vendor events can be an incredible source of leads if you learn how to work the booth properly. (And by the way, that's where most consultants go wrong. They think doing what they see everybody else doing at a vendor event is the most effective way to work a booth, and they are dead wrong.)

So let's start with a quick review of the way to work the "system" of this business.

I call that system "Lather-Rinse-Repeat:"

I'm sure you're asking: Why is this Important? Because if you follow this process - it makes the business easy. Don't follow it and you make the business hard.

Here's my "lather-rinse-repeat" process. It should be completed in order:

1) Connect with your connections or network to generate leads, and meet new prospects. (When you meet prospects at a booth – spend time getting to know them.)

2) Once you've connected, show them your products and get them excited about your products. (Great time to make a wish list.)

3) Explain your awesome hostess rewards and ask them to book a party.

4) Once they are booked, coach your hostesses well.

5) Do an Effective Presentation at your parties (an effective presentation will result in high sales, new parties booked, and prospects for the business)

6) There are 2 or 3 hot prospects at every party. Schedule "coffee connections" or virtual meetings with these prospects to share the information about the business.

7) Sponsor those who are interested - and be a great coach and mentor. Train them well.

REPEAT!

Applying the "Lather-Rinse-Repeat" Process at Vendor Events:

When you're working a booth – you are focused on the first 3 parts of this process:

1) Making Connections / Generating Leads
2) Getting these leads excited about your products or services
3) Asking them to book a party.

And it's important to learn how to "work this system" in this order.

If you don't – for example, if someone walks by your booth and you ask them to book a party without connecting (which is step one), or without knowing if they are excited about your products (which is step two) – you are simply making your business difficult.

I learned this the hard way.

I've always used vendor events (especially Women's Expos) as a lead generating activity for my business.

The first few years, I worked my booths the way I observed others working their booths.

You know – I offered a big prize drawing, stopped people walking past my booth by sticking a clipboard with a drawing slip in their face, handed out hundreds of dollars' worth of catalogs, and went home – often with 400-to-500 drawing slips. I mistakenly thought these drawing slips were really good leads, since they often checked those boxes that said, "Yes, I want to earn free merchandise by booking a party," or "Yes, I'd like to learn more about the business."

In hindsight, most checked those boxes because they "thought" it would give them a better shot at being chosen for the prize.

Working a booth can be exhausting. But I would force myself to start making calls – first, to everyone who indicated they wanted to book a party.

At first, I attacked the project enthusiastically. But that follow-up was taking dozens of hours, and was producing very little for my business.

Sure – I booked a party or two.

But based on the amount of time and energy it was taking to do those follow-ups, compared to my results – it was a very costly endeavor.

Remember – time is your most valuable asset. So you always want to consider how you spend your precious time very carefully.

The "300 Drawing Slip Experiment"

A friend told me about doing this – so I copied her "experiment."

For a couple months, I went to every vendor event I could find – women's expos, a county fair, and some business events sponsored by a Chamber of Commerce.

At each event, I went to every single direct sales company and filled out their drawing slip. I checked both the "book a party" and the "learn about the business" boxes on every slip.

During the "experiment" I filled out about 300 slips.

Guess how many of those consultants called me or followed up with me?

The results were actually alarming.

Only one consultant – just one – followed-up. She sent me one email (that I didn't answer, on purpose to see what happened next), and I never heard from her again.

So my question for you is, "Are YOU doing thorough and effective follow-up on those drawing slips?"

Based on that experiment – if you are – then I commend you because you are truly an exception, not the rule.

The follow-up is frustrating – not fun. But if you're focusing on generating leads by collecting drawing slips – it's the only way to get a return on both your money and time.

After several years of working vendor events, and continually being frustrated with the follow-up process; I had an experience that caused me to "flip my switch" and completely change how I worked my booths.

I had booked a very expensive booth (my investment was about $1500 after the booth rental fee, carpeting, etc.) at a Women's Expo in Minneapolis, and I took a quick bathroom break.

As I was exiting the restroom, I deposited my used towel into the trash can, and there…staring up at me from the trash…was one of my catalogs.

It felt like that catalog reached out of the trash can and slapped me across the face. It felt like a personal insult.

I slumped back to my booth, feeling discouraged and frustrated, and **made a huge decision in that moment.**

I was never going to hand out a catalog at a vendor event again.

In fact, I made a decision that day, that I was either going to figure out how to get huge returns on both the money I invested renting a booth, and on the time I invested working the booth, or I would stop working them completely.

Most of all – I set a goal that I would work a booth so effectively that I would go home with booked parties on my calendar. That way, I could eliminate all of that frustrating time I was spending (and losing) with follow-up calls, emails, and text messages.

And that's exactly what I did.

After some careful thought, and some trial and error -- I completely changed the way I work a booth, and it works.

- I stopped handing out a single catalog.
- I don't put out any business cards for people to take.
- I stopped holding any type of drawings or contests.
- I do not try to sell any of my products (by the way, not selling products helps me book more parties).

These changes eliminated a lot of expense and simplified the way I work my booth. They also put me in the driver's seat with new leads.

Now I have one single, focused goal at a booth: **Book Parties**

My system for working the booth to accomplish my goal – booking parties -- really works.

It works so well, that at one women's expo (this was a 4-day event, and it probably had at least 10,000 attendees – so I do want you to keep that in perspective), I booked 21 parties. 17 of them held.

At the end of that weekend, I packed up my booth, headed home, and rather than dreading all the frustrating follow-up calls – I took a hot bubble bath and celebrated my success.

The only calls and connections I had to make the following week were for hostess coaching.

And most of all – I had fun working that booth. Business should be fun!

My Book Parties at the Booth System:

Before I dive into the details about how I NOW work a booth (sharing my new and improved system that gets results – meaning bookings – right AT the booth), I need to preface it by saying there's a lot that "should" be considered before you choose to shell out your hard-earned dollars and dedicate your incredibly valuable time.

Unfortunately, most consultants simply ask, "how much is it," and make their choices for vendor events based on the cost, versus the really important criteria.

(I have an entire training course on working vendor events well called "How to Get Outrageous Results Working Vendor Events and Women's Expos" that walks you through every detail for choosing events well, setting up your booth properly, attracting attendees into your booth, giving presentations to attract a mob, using booths with your current customers and hostesses – and much more.)

I'm going to assume that you've made a good choice of vendor events for this training.

You've also set-up your booth well so attendees can touch, or feel, or smell, or taste your products – or they can "come into your booth" as though it is your mini-retail store.

You are standing in your booth (Never sit behind a table. You want to be at "eye level" with your guests. Wear comfortable shoes, and change your shoes throughout the day.)

You're going to stop people by starting conversations.

(Reminder: This is Step 1 in the business "lather-rinse-repeat" process.)

You AREN'T going to say, "Have you heard of our company?"

Instead, you are going to observe and ask questions.

For example, a woman walks by with pink hair.

You say, "I love your hair – what inspired you to dye it this gorgeous pink?" (Note – that's a compliment and a question.)

Or three women walk by wearing matching jackets.

You could say, "Hi ladies. I couldn't help but notice that you're all wearing the same jacket. What's that all about?"

This is the start of building a connection by taking a sincere interest in others.

Everyone has an interesting story, if you're willing to take a sincere interest and ask enough questions. Everyone.

You can't rush the relationship.

Eventually, the person might ask about your products. Or, eventually you can transition the discussion; but you have to continue to ask questions.

(I'm sure you've seen it – where the person at a booth has a "memorized commercial" about their products, and the second they start spewing it out – it's as though they don't even come up for air. They just keep talking and talking and talking. I get exhausted just watching them, and they certainly aren't keeping me engaged.)

Let me give you an example that can help explain this...

My former company sold women's clothing. We had sashes that could be used creatively in many different ways – belts, scarves, headbands, etc.

I used to hold one of the sashes in my hand at the booth.

Often, as I was getting to know a guest, they would ask me, "What is that?"

I would hand it to them and say, "It's a sash. Feel this!"

But…I always want to "put the ball back into their court" and keep the conversation going…so I would say, "How does it feel?"

They usually responded with some sort of comment about it being "soft, comfortable, etc."

Then I'd drop a booking bid (you know, those simple statements that help you explain the benefits of hosting a party) I'd say, "At our parties, I usually show the guests five or six ways to work with our sashes."

And then…NO, I DIDN'T ASK HER TO BOOK…YET…I asked another question so I could learn more about this prospective hostess.

(Remember – Step 2 in the process is getting the person excited about your products. I want hostesses who have big wish lists because they will work at having a successful party!)

Next, I'd point them over to the table where I had all of our sashes laid out to show the colors in our current collection.

I'd ask, "Which of these colors do you like the best?"

Some would say, "black," some would pull out their personal color charts to see which would be best for them.

I'd continue to ask questions about them.

Do they work outside the home?

If yes, what did they do?

If no, what did they do?

Do they travel a lot (because our clothes were great for traveling)? If yes, for business or fun?

What have been some of their favorite places during their travels?

You get the idea…

Based on what I learned about them, I would focus them on the outfits that I had hanging around my booth.

Then I'd ask, "Which outfits would be best for (your job, your trips, being a stay at home Mom, etc.)?

They would steer me towards their favorite outfit (see how much information you get from people when you simply ask?).

The Price Question

At some point during our conversation, most prospects will ask about price.

I LOVE this question!!

Note: Most consultants mess this up because they simply haven't been trained.

When your prospect asks, "How much is this jacket?" or "How much is this outfit?"...(or in your case, "How much is ___?) you don't answer immediately.

Instead, (and remember the formula), you compliment them, and explain features and benefits.

Example:

"Rosemary, you have great taste because you've chosen one of our most popular outfits. Let me show you why women love this so much."

Then, I'm going to go through some features AND benefits.

Example:

"This jacket is made from our special poly/cotton blend, so it can be thrown in the washing machine. You'll save a fortune on your dry cleaning bill.

It has pockets on the side – great for your cell phone or car keys.

The cuffs have a wide hem, so you can fold them over and roll them up.

Plus, the jacket comes in six different colors."

And then I will answer the price question.

"This jacket is JUST $89."

(I've just pointed out all the amazing attributes of the jacket, so yes, it is "JUST" $89.)

But here's what you need to ask next:

"How does that sound to you?"

She will either say, "It sounds like a great deal" or "It is out of my budget" – right?

If she thinks it's a really reasonable price (and by the way, about 70% of your prospects will think it's a great price, after you've explained all the features and benefits), then you say:

"If I can show you a way that you could actually get it at a huge discount – or possibly for FREE – would you be interested to learn more?"

That's when you explain your hostess rewards.

For the person who thinks the jacket price is beyond their budget, you say, "I truly appreciate you sharing that with me.

"If I can show you a way that you could actually get it at a huge discount – or possibly for FREE – would you be interested to learn more?"

(Yes – it's exactly the same question, no matter what their response is to the price. That's why this is so easy!)

Next, you give a brief overview of your hostess rewards. Show them the page in your catalog that explains free merchandise and earning credits. Show them your current hostess specials and exclusives.

Then you ask the question:

"How would you feel about booking a party to get that outfit free, or at a significant discount?"

Some will say "yes," some will have some "speed bumps" that you'll need to help them solve.

And then, you'll use my "Secret Booking Weapon" to help you get your prospect booked on your calendar.

It's a special tool I developed, that I use at booths, that helps me get a hostess booked right there at the booth.

It's a huge, poster-sized calendar.

(GO TO: DirectSalesDaily.com/booking-calendar to download a copy of the file. You can get it printed for about $5)

Before I explain how to use this tool, I need to talk about incentives.

I don't want you to think you need to give extra booking gifts or incentives at your parties (or in most situations!). Usually when I see a consultant who is offering additional "bribes" for bookings, she hasn't really mastered her booking skills. (That's a completely different course!)

But there are SOME situations – and working vendor events is one of them – where it makes very good sense to offer additional incentives for your prospects to take action.

There is an entire video that explains how to set-up your booking calendar, when you download it.

Basically, you are going to label the calendar "Booking Special," you are going to cross off any dates (using a post-it note) that are "booked" – whether you are booked with a party, a doctor's appointment, or date night. You are "booked."

On your available dates, you will be offering a Gift Certificate, that your hostess can use in addition to her hostess credits, when she hosts a qualifying party (whatever that amount is for your company), AND keeps her date.

This is important.

It needs to be clear that this extra incentive for booking a party is strictly available for those who book right there at the event.

Don't be cheap here. You need to offer an amount (I always started at a $50 gift certificate) that is enough of an incentive to get them to commit to the party right there, on the spot.

Here's what I say:

I've explained the hostess rewards and benefits, and I've asked this prospect to book a party. We've discussed any of her "speed bumps" that might be causing her to hesitate.

And then I say…

"I also have a very special surprise – strictly for people who book parties right here at this event.

I don't know if you noticed my Booking Special?

(It's a 2' x 3' poster, on an easel, near the front of your booth so they'd have to be nearly blind to miss it. But that's beside the point.)

WHEN you book your party on one of these dates (and I only offer dates for the upcoming five weeks), you will get a special $50 gift certificate to use, in addition to all the other hostess rewards, on the night of your party.

Look – my calendar is filling fast. (You walk her over to your booking calendar.) Do any of these dates work for you – because I'd love for you to get this additional special."

Any prospect who is strongly considering booking a party will scramble to get that extra special.

If someone says, "I need to check my calendar" or "I need to check with my friends," you can respond with:

"Rosemary, I totally understand. But considering how quickly my calendar, and this additional special, is being booked – why don't we pencil in a date, and I will call you first thing next week to confirm it. That way, I can honor the booth special, and you won't get locked out."

I literally pull out my pencil to write her date on my calendar. I take out my post-it notepad, write "booked" on a post-it, and put it on my "booking calendar" on the date she chose. (I do all of those things to solidify her commitment.)

Next, I schedule a time that I will call her to confirm (or if she is solid on her date, the time for our first hostess coaching call).

I even give this new booked hostess a simple "certificate" (simply a document that I send home with their date/time and the amount they will receive when they meet the requirements – there's a sample in my vendor event course) to take home.

Depending on how quickly their date is coming up, I will either send her hostess packet home with her, or I will mail it to her.

My "secret booking weapon" calendar is a great visual tool that helps you put bookings on your calendar right at your booth when you use it properly.

It's not going to do all the work for you.

It is part of your "process" for connecting, getting women excited about your products, then explaining hostess rewards, and then asking them to book.

It is a closing tool. It's an incentive that encourages your prospects to take action right there, on the spot.

The first time I used it, I was directly across from a booth of Mary Kay consultants. It was working so well, that they came over and took pictures of it so they could use the concept at future events.

Keep things in perspective!

A couple months ago, one of my students sent me an email, after using these techniques at a vendor event.

She said she booked one party.

I was concerned, because in my experience, the only time this doesn't work is when consultants make changes, and mess it up.

(For example, they only offer a $10 gift certificate; or they offer the hostess a choice of some of their inventory, etc.)

So I reached out by phone to find out what happened.

She said, "Susie, this was a really small event. It was only a couple hours long, and there wasn't any traffic. I was thrilled that I came home with a party booked – especially since I had NEVER booked a party from a vendor event in the past."

I can only imagine what kind of results she will get when she uses these techniques and tools at a better event.

In Conclusion...

When you choose to book a vendor event – your results will be a direct reflection of how you "work" the booth.

Most of all – business should be fun. You'll get the best results at a vendor event when you have fun meeting some incredible people, and if you work the process right, you'll book some NEW hostesses on your calendar!

That feels great!

Ready to learn more?

If working vendor events is part of your lead generation strategy, then it's important to get a good return on both your money and your time.

To learn more about my full course, go to:

DirectSalesDaily.com/courses

Want more of this type of training?

These are some of the additional books in my Business Builder Book series:

(go to: DirectSalesDaily.com/books for all the details and publishing dates - or check them out on Amazon or Kindle)

1) How to Have an Awesome Launch Party
2) How to Book Parties at Vendor Events
3) How to Re-Launch Your Business
4) How to Use Fundraisers to Fill Your Calendar with Bookings
5) How to Book Parties – AT Your Parties
6) How to Connect with 2 or 3 Hot Business Prospects at Every Party
7) How to Have Awesome Prospects Connections – then Close!
8) How to Get the Most from Company Opportunity Events
9) Your Step-by-Step Hostess Coaching Guide
10) How to Turn Hot Hostesses Into Fabulous Team Members
11) How to Get Sales, Bookings and Prospects from Customer Care Calls
12) How to Double – Even Triple – Your Sales at Every Single Party
13) How to Have Highly Productive Virtual Parties
14) Networking 101
15) Online Lead Generation
16) How to Get Every New Team Member Off to a Great Start
17) Your Team Communications Plan

18) What to Do When Your Team Members Get Stuck
19) How to Earn Your First Promotion
20) How to Sponsor Long Distance Consultants Effectively
21) Smart Leaders Promote Strong Leaders
22) Building to the Top Without Working 24/7

Look for my other books on Amazon or Kindle:

"I Did It, and You Can, Too: How to Build a Six Figure Business in Just 15 Hours Per Week."

"The Pros and Cons of Building More Than One Direct Sales Business: What You Must Consider Before You Join a Second (or Third!) Company"

"8 Weeks to Your Promotion"

"From Drowning in Debt to Financial Freedom: How to Bail Yourself Out of a Financial Mess by Building a Home Party or Network Marketing Business."

"How to Choose the Best Direct Sales Company for You"

"How to Build a $1 Million+ Organization in Just 12 Months"

Susie Nelson is a coach, trainer, and business growth strategist for direct sales consultants and start-up companies.

She built an empire in a home party business - achieving every possible goal that the company offered:

- 2nd National Sales Manager in the Company (the top level in the company at the time - only 6 Managers ever achieved this level).
- Built a Million Dollar+ Sales Organization
- Earned the "Circle of Excellence" recognition every year (for unit sales of $650,000+)
- Promoted the most leaders of anyone in the U.S. company (16 directly, 2 indirectly)
- Honored with the company's "President's Award" twice
- Built and maintained a six figure income (for 11 years straight)

Susie is the author of many books for home party and direct sales consultants - available through Amazon and Kindle.

She has worked on the corporate side of the business with several start-up companies.

Susie has literally helped thousands of consultants improve their businesses and make more money, as a result of what they implemented.

To contact Susie:

Email: Susie@SusieNelson-Training.com

32817750R00020

Made in the USA
Middletown, DE
08 January 2019